# Contents

Minus 60 degrees Fahrenheit; the orange glow is a product of the low-hanging March sun.

~ Chapter 1

THE ULTIMATE PHOTOGRAPH

The leader of the wolf pack glanced back at me as I scrambled after him across the ice. He didn't appear to sense any danger. He just looked curious, maybe even a little amused, as if saying to himself, "*That* odd creature is really trying to sneak up on *me?*"

It was crazy to think that anyone bundled up in Arctic gear could escape a wolf's notice. Wolves are one of the most perceptive animals on earth, with extraordinary senses. But I couldn't help myself. My heart pounded with excitement because I sensed something about this wolf, whom I had nicknamed Buster (after my father). He was about to present me with the chance to take the greatest photograph of my life.

Buster was leading the pack to a favorite spot, an iceberg on which they often spent their time exploring, howling with one another, goofing off, napping. Since it was April, the wolves' iceberg was still shackled to the land by an eight-foot crust of ice. The altitude is irresistible to Arctic wolves. They seem to *like* climbing to the tops of things. From the heights, they can survey the territory and keep an eye on new developments. They had littered the iceberg with droppings—a KEEP OUT sign to other packs. And to me.

Looking for tracks in full Arctic gear,
which includes handmade Inuit mukluks.

Now I needed to find my perfect vantage point, too. As I crouched and lumbered across the dry, Arctic snow, it squeaked like Styrofoam under my feet. The wolves were some 150 yards away from me. So I settled against a six-foot pressure (ice) ridge and began to shoot photographs frantically. My powerful lenses made the wolves appear much closer than they were. As I reloaded my camera, Buster trotted over to a flat projection halfway up the iceberg. From this makeshift throne, he watched me. Suddenly, a single shaft of light illuminated the wolf while leaving the surrounding iceberg in blue, muted shadow. Nature had never provided me with a more perfectly composed photograph.

Buster sat there, in that perfect spot, for no more than thirty seconds. My thoughts raced ahead to when the editors at *National Geographic* would process my film. I was nervous and pessimistic about the outcome. Had the wind shaken the lens at the last second? Were the wolf's eyes open, or did I catch him blinking at the instant I snapped the shutter?

I found out later that, out of dozens of shots I'd taken of the lone wolf, only one turned out the way I had hoped it might.

Good photographs, like wolves, are elusive. Good photographs *of* wolves? Nearly impossible. I took this humbling realization as a challenge, which would inspire me in the long months to come.

Many people think Alaska is the most northerly part of North America, but Ellesmere Island, located in Canada's Northwest Territories, is actually several hundred miles farther north than any part of Alaska. From Ellesmere's tip to the North Pole measures some 500 miles across the Arctic Ocean.

During the winter, and for the first fifty or so days of "spring," such as it is, the water is frozen six to eight feet thick

Ice patterns shot from a plane over the Arctic Ocean.

Facing page: The perfect shot.

Fellow adventurer, Will Steger.

Facing page: The wolves have had no reason to fear humans on their remote island.

most of the way to the Pole. But this ice is nothing like the glassy ice familiar to skaters. Across its craggy, snow-blown surface, the ice cap is wrinkled with pressure ridges that make traveling on it difficult. Even worse are the frequent "leads"—yawning cracks in the ice that reveal open seawater.

I had taken other journeys into this treacherous, beautiful region during the first twenty years of my photographic career. Still, the *National Geographic* assignment to photograph the wildlife of Ellesmere Island, especially the wolves, was the fulfillment of a dream. And it all started when I first met my friend and fellow dreamer Will Steger. I think we each sensed something in the other: a kinship, a vision of the way we wanted to live our lives. Both of us had dreamed since childhood about testing ourselves, about danger, and about discovery. And we had found adventure wherever we could manage it.

The part of our conversation that I remember most vividly was about wolves. Arctic wolves. He had been dogsledding on Ellesmere with his wife two summers earlier. One morning they received a visitor.

"We woke up," Will told me, "and this large white head was staring at us through the flap of our tent. An Arctic wolf, as close to me as you are now. He showed no fear. He followed us for days, played with our dogs."

I was thrilled to think that a pack might exist that hadn't learned to fear humans. The images of that white wolf peering into Will Steger's tent and later playing with his dogs stuck stubbornly in my mind until I finally returned on assignment for *National Geographic* to follow the lives of these wolves for the whole Arctic summer. Even now, this time remains a highlight of my career, of my life.

The rocky outcropping at the den's entrance has been carved for eons by the winds of the High Arctic.

☙ Chapter 2

MEETING THE FAMILY

Adult wolf standing on the rooftop of the den.

One of my first concerns was about how much I might interfere with the lives of these wolves. Would my presence cause them to abandon their den and disappear?

During most of the year, a wolf pack roams over its entire territory, making wolf study almost impossible. But each spring, the pack stays in or near one place. The mother must take to the den to have her pups, and the behavior of the whole pack revolves around feeding their young and ensuring their safety. This phenomenon makes study easier, but it also is a uniquely sensitive time.

How could I make it clear to the pack that I meant them no harm? That I would keep my distance and simply observe?

At first, I did not set up a permanent campsite in case the pack fled and moved to another den. I approached the den cautiously, alert to any signs that my presence might be causing stress in the pack. But the wolves never appeared overly nervous or bothered.

The den was set high on a hill. At its opening, rocks formed a kind of porch on which the pack members spent much of their time. The den opened into the earth from an entryway just large enough to fit snugly around the mother wolf. A hungry polar bear,

The pups' narrow view of the world as seen from inside the den.

in other words, could not squeeze in to make a snack out of the growing pups. Inside, a clean, bug-free layer of sand covered the ground leading into a cave twenty feet deep. The rock walls provided excellent protection from the bitter cold.

Pups spend their first weeks inside the den huddled around their mother, and each other, for warmth. I was eager and impatient for my first look at them. When they finally appeared outside the den, they proved well worth the wait.

There were six puppies, cute little gray bundles of fur waddling after the adults on short, fuzzy legs and oversized paws. I guessed that they were about five weeks old. It seemed impossible that by winter they'd be running alongside their parents.

Several days later, I set up a camera about fifty yards from the den and was shooting photographs of the wriggling ball of pups. All seven adults looked in my direction, stretched, howled a few

The first lone excursion of one young pup.

8

The pups study the world outside their den.

times at the sky, and took off on a hunt. I couldn't believe it! Not one adult stayed behind to bark at me and keep me away from the den. They trusted me with their precious pups. Finally, after all those frustrating years of wolf pursuit, I would be able to get close to an entire pack. And what a family it was!

The way adult wolves are constantly caring for the young in their pack is only one of many similarities with human families. Wolves mate for life, and the whole pack functions as an extended family of aunts and uncles, brothers and sisters. They take turns baby-sitting and teaching the pups what they need to know.

Wolves have very individual personalities. Bison and musk-oxen all behave much the same within their herds. Not wolves. It probably has to do with their intelligence and gifts of perception.

At first, however, *my* perceptions were not up to the task of

The adult wolves are excellent caretakers of their young charges.

10

Scruffy is the lowest-ranking member of the adult hierarchy, but he basks in the respect and adoration of the pups.

Buster, the alpha male, sniffs a bouquet of Arctic poppies.

telling the seven wolves in this pack apart. But over the weeks of watching and listening to the wolves, I found myself more and more aware of their differences, like body scars, facial expressions, and coloring.

I also noticed that some of them behaved in dominant ways, bristling and cocky. Others were more submissive, cringing when in the presence of a "superior" and always trying to keep the peace. In other words, a hierarchy became apparent, a ranking of the wolves according to their power in relation to the others.

At the top was the alpha male, Buster. He was usually first to attack on a hunt and the first to eat after a kill. Buster's eyes were extremely expressive. Sometimes they were piercing, threatening. Other times they were amused, haughty, or quizzical. Weighing less than 100 pounds, he was not the largest of the pack. But he stood proudly on thin, long legs, taller than even the largest German shepherd.

Nearly his equal was the alpha female. I called her Midback because of a trail of dark fur running down her back. She was probably the most intelligent pack member. It was also clear that she was the *least* pleased to have me around. Midback's quickness and skill made her the best hunter among the pack.

Although scientists say that only the alpha pair has pups each spring, Midback was not the mother of the pups. There is no way to know why this alpha female did not give birth, but she was the most fiercely protective "parent" the pups had. She behaved like a dominant aunt who was often jealous of the pups' mother, whom I called, simply, Mom. Midback often rivaled Mom's authority over the pups.

Mom quickly became one of my favorites. She was a natural mother—gentle, tolerant, and devoted to the pups. Her facial expression can only be described as sweet and serene. And for some

Midback, the pack's best hare hunter, catches her prey and carries it with haughty pride to the grateful pups.

reason she seemed to have complete trust in humans. Maybe she simply got used to having me around because she was tied to the den.

The other wolf that could most often be found with the pups was my other favorite. He was an "adolescent" wolf, probably from the previous year's litter. His position in the pack was at the opposite end from the alpha pair—the bottom. I called him Scruffy because he was always a mess. His summer coat was scraggly, with huge balls of hair hanging from virtually every part of his hide.

There was a kind of goofiness about Scruffy that endeared him to me, especially since he tended to follow me around a lot. He was usually left behind from a hunt, but baby-sitting was the perfect job for him because of his playfulness. It also gave him the

At times, the usually playful Scruffy must show his dominance over the pups by exposing his teeth and growling.

chance to act dominantly over somebody, at least when Mom wasn't looking.

It was part of his job to play rough with the pups, knock them down hard enough to make them yelp. Though this kind of bullying may seem cruel, it is a necessary part of the pups' training. They have to learn the importance of knowing one's place in the hierarchy. This arrangement is crucial to the pack's unity and survival. Maintaining that ranking and its strict rules of behavior keeps the peace, avoids continual fights and injuries, maybe even death.

I knew less about the remaining three adults in the pack, mostly because they spent less time at the den site. Left Shoulder, a male named for a three-inch patch of missing fur on his left shoulder, was the largest, whitest wolf in the pack. Despite his size, he was submissive to the point of groveling in the presence of both Buster and Midback. The other two adults had even lower status in the pack, and I never got much of a sense of their personalities.

Many changes in the pack's membership would inevitably follow from one year to the next. But these seven adults and six pups made up the "family" as it existed one particular spring and summer on Ellesmere Island.

Facing page: Left Shoulder shows no sign of favoring the wounded shoulder for which he was named; the wound was probably caused by the horn or hoof of a musk-ox.

16

≥ Chapter 3

LIVING AS NEIGHBORS

While searching for an ideal campsite, I found a skull embedded in the powdery soil.

The story the skull told of the wolf's amazing survival skills intrigued me. Puncturing the lower jawbone was the tip of a musk-ox horn that had broken off, probably during combat. Bone tissue had grown thick across the point of injury, showing that he had lived for at least several months after the battle. The simple act of chewing must have been terribly painful, but his worn teeth indicated that he was very old when he died.

The discovery of this skull gave me an unusual glimpse into the harsh lives these wolves lead. It also provided a symbolic site on which to stake my own territorial claim for the spring and summer.

This setting was a deep valley about a quarter-mile east of the den. A pair of binoculars allowed me to keep track of the pack's activities. My presence did not seem to affect the wolves in a negative way. They made regular trips to the camp, apparently to satisfy their curiosity. My goal was to blend in, to lie low without trying to hide or trick the wolves. There was, however, one unavoidable exception to this approach. It was my means of transportation, the Suzuki all-terrain vehicle (ATV).

Facing page: Scruffy baby-sits puppies by the den's entrance.

I used this four-wheel buggy to carry my equipment and to keep up with the free-roaming pack. It's nothing for a wolf to travel forty miles at a steady pace of six miles per hour. It would have been impossible to keep up with them on foot.

Most of my time, of course, was spent not on the ATV but loitering within camera range of the den. Since the sun was up twenty-four hours a day at this point, I didn't think—or sleep—in night-and-day patterns. Besides, the wolves did not appear to have any regular sleep patterns either. As with their diet and hunting, wolves take opportunities when and where they can; they seem to know when it makes sense to be asleep and when it makes sense to be awake.

Often I found myself staying up twenty hours or more at a stretch, fearful that if I did fall asleep, the wolves would do something never before documented and I'd miss it. I would grab my sleeping bag and telephoto lens and curl up on the hillside overlooking the den, taking catnaps and every now and then cocking an ear or raising an eyelid toward the activity across the way.

More than once I fell asleep in spite of myself, only to wake

The pack completely accepted my presence in their territory.

Despite their deadly earnest struggle for survival, the wolves find a surprising amount of time for play.

to the curious sniffing of a wolf a few yards away. It was satisfying, at these times, to know that the creatures whom I was observing were keeping a similarly watchful eye on me.

A few words here about anthropomorphism, the common practice of giving human characteristics and feelings to non-humans. Throughout my career—even when I've felt closest to my wild subjects—I've always tried to preserve a boundary between us.

Yet, animals undoubtedly have more feelings than we give them credit for. To ignore this fact, or view their emotional range as smaller, *inferior* to ours, is just as wrong as thinking of them in strictly human terms.

I genuinely believe a magic exists in creatures as perceptive and intelligent as wolves, a magic that we may not be able to observe or measure in any scientific way.

Sometimes, during those days on Ellesmere, I would wonder how the wolves perceived me. Maybe they attributed wolflike feelings to my odd human behaviors. I wouldn't have been surprised.

The puppies were even willing to pose for me.

21

Pack members during the white-out of an Arctic blizzard.

~ Chapter 4

ADAPTATION

During a high Arctic winter, the sun does not appear for four months and temperatures can drop to minus seventy degrees Fahrenheit. Add fierce winds, and you have a climate that seems unsuited to any living creature. But the process of evolution produces characteristics in animals that allow them to adapt to the environment in which they live.

No matter how cold I felt it to be, I never observed a wolf who acted chilled. I suspect that even in the middle of the harshest winter Arctic wolves find a way to keep themselves comfortable. They probably spend much of their time in the position I saw them sleep in—curled up into tight balls with their bushy tails draped protectively over their noses. This position exposes the smallest possible amount of body surface to the cold.

Since wolves appear to prefer sleeping outside, their winter coats and "leggings" must be superbly insulated. Their legs look twice as thick in winter as they do in summer. And they even grow long hair on the bottoms of their feet, which almost hides their footpads.

As warmer weather approaches, the wolves begin to shed. At one point or another, all the wolves had great gobs of shedding undercoat trailing up to two feet behind them. All summer, I

Midback, the pack's alpha female and best hunter, moves with self-assured deliberation.

23

The pack's messiest and neatest members: Scruffy (right) and Left Shoulder (below).

waited for the moment when all the old excess hair would be gone and the wolves would be sleek and smooth. But such a day never came. The next winter's fur started growing in before the last one's could be entirely shaken or scraped free.

This messiness doesn't mean, however, that the wolves did not care about keeping themselves clean. Maintaining their white coats, of course, is necessary because it provides their camouflage during the winter. But they displayed individual differences, too, in how well-groomed they kept themselves. Left Shoulder and Scruffy represented the two extremes: The older wolf was always whiter, prettier than the rest, while Scruffy lived up to his nickname.

Buster, the alpha male, was another of the tidier individuals. This trait became evident in one of the most remarkable scenes I have ever witnessed in the animal world. Buster had turned almost black with mud in pursuit of an Arctic hare, but rather than lying down immediately to enjoy his meal, he took a long, careful swim, after which he shook himself dry—all with the dead hare clamped in his jaw. Only then did he sit down to his meal.

Another example of superb adaptation to environment is the wolf's legendary sense of smell. Some scientists have estimated that wolves can smell thousands of times better than humans can. Their snouts are always cocked in the direction of the prevailing breeze because it provides such important information about their world, especially the location of potential prey. Heavy winds, however, seem to annoy them with too much random information, and they avoid hunting altogether on such days.

On one occasion, I followed several of the wolves to a nearby beach where a dead fish had washed up on the shore. It had been dead for some time, and it smelled quite rank. The wolves took turns rolling around on the fish until they all shared in the stench. This behavior seemed odd to me, until they took off on their hunt. Evidently, they were masking their own scent so that a musk-ox or caribou could be reassured that it was only a dead fish stalking it, nothing dangerous.

The wolves' eyesight and hearing are in many ways as impressive as their sense of smell. Once it took me several minutes, *with* my binoculars, to detect an Arctic hare that Buster's eyes had been following for some time.

Their excellent senses allow these animals to do more than just locate prey efficiently. Wolves are probably one of the most social animals outside of the primates. The success of the pack depends strongly on a highly developed system of communication with neighboring packs as well as between individual pack members. Smell, vision, and hearing play crucial roles in such communication.

Young Arctic hares; they will grow to weigh up to 12 pounds and be camouflaged by their white fur.

A big hunt begins with a howling reveille.

Puppies begin to practice howling very early in life; their amusing, high-pitched efforts add to the family songfest.

The most well-known form of communication wolves use is their howl. Howling begins at a very early age. Within weeks after emerging from the den, the pups cock their tiny snouts to the sky right alongside their parents.

I was often able to watch and listen to a songfest by the whole pack. Each had his or her distinctive voice and a preferred range of notes. Midback, for instance, had a high-pitched, almost whiny cry, whereas Left Shoulder would howl in the lower octaves.

Whatever their preferred notes, however, one thing was certain. Every wolf avoided hitting the same note as any of its packmates. When this happened by accident, one of the voices would frantically shuffle about until discord could be achieved once again. This phenomenon apparently has evolved to suit the scattered distribution of the Arctic wolves across an unfriendly environment, not always in safe numbers. With as many different tones as possible in its howling, a pack can give the impression of greater size and can intimidate possible intruders. I know I have been fooled by a distant pack's howls, estimating its size to be double what it turns out to be when I come across its members.

Wolves howl for many reasons beyond signaling their location to other packs. When part of the pack is off hunting, they howl to those left behind, perhaps letting them know their position. Wolves also will howl after a long sleep. Such howling seems to work up the group into enthusiasm for the next hunt, much as a team of athletes will shout in unison before a big game. But whatever practical purposes the wolves' howling might serve, it also seems to be for pleasure.

Midback wakes up ready to hunt and howls to rouse her packmates.

❦ Chapter 5

THE HUNT

After you live with wolves for a while, you can sense when something big is about to happen. One day, I quickly realized that I was about to witness such an event in the wolves' lives.

Except for the occasional playful times with the pups, adult wolves divide most of their time between sleeping and hunting. When they've been sleeping a long time, it's likely that a major hunt will follow, and this particular day I had spent endless chilly hours alone, watching the wolves sleep under the midnight sun. When I could hardly keep my eyes open another minute, I started to pack up my cameras and head back to camp. But just then the alpha female awoke and began to howl.

It wasn't long before the whole pack was up and joining with her in high-pitched howls. The ritual also included long, deep canine stretching to loosen sleep-stiffened muscles.

For ten minutes the wake-up continued as sluggishness gave way to a building excitement, theirs and mine. Then, suddenly, Midback took off toward the east, quickly followed by a single-file parade of all the other adults in the pack. At the speed they were going, I knew they would quickly be out of sight.

I ran back to camp and began to gather together enough food

Facing page: Two adults rest in cotton grass; in the balmy atmosphere, it is almost possible to forget about the swift and inevitable advance of winter.

and extra fuel for what I expected to be a long trip. Since the wolves regularly disappeared for days at a time, I had no idea how long we'd be gone. Even though I was able to load my gear into my ATV in less than ten minutes, the pack had already disappeared. Heading in the direction they'd taken, I drove up to thirty miles per hour for about seven miles before coming to a high ridge. From there, I could finally see the wolves through my binoculars.

Wildly uneven ground makes travel on wheels very difficult, but it does not slow down wolves. When I did finally catch up with them, I hung off to the side, making it easier for the wolves to ignore me. Occasionally they would close ranks around me, and, for those few miles, I would allow myself the exhilarating feeling of being a pack member. But just as I was beginning to get into a kind of hunting wolf mind-set, they would veer off again, leaving me scrambling to keep them in range.

Several miles later, their march became more direct, as though they knew exactly where they were going. Realizing that an encounter might await us over the next ridge, I decided to race ahead. I wanted to have my cameras ready to go.

Sure enough, a half-mile ahead I saw nearly a dozen musk-oxen grazing. The herd, which included three calves, was scattered across the broad, grassy valley.

Moments after I had set up my tripod, the wolves appeared on the top of the rise. With Midback taking the lead, they first crept forward slowly, then gradually increased their pace until they were charging down the hillside in an attempt to catch the herd off guard.

The wolves were halfway down the slope before the musk-oxen saw them. The oxen rushed toward one another and gathered into a ring just as the wolves arrived. The three calves were inside the circle, protected and out of sight. It did not seem to me that

Facing page: The wolves test a herd of musk-oxen in hopes of finding a vulnerable member.

30

A stand-off between an Arctic wolf and a circle of musk-oxen.

Hooves and horns are deadly weapons; the wolves must take extreme care to avoid injury.

the adults in this herd were panicking. Their dull-eyed watchfulness seemed to say that this was just another unpleasant encounter with wolves.

After fanning out and circling, the wolves charged a few times, but the musk-oxen held their ground. A few times the lead musk-ox ventured out to challenge the alpha male wolf, face-to-face, then returned to its circle.

Wolves have been known to pick away at a herd for a full day, wearing them down and making them nervous long enough to destroy the herd's strategy. But with so many horned adults to deal with, the wolves' chances for success looked slim to me. The wolves seemed to agree. They chose to give up before wasting much more precious energy. I was just starting to pack up my gear when events took an abrupt turn.

As the wolves were trotting away, the herd bolted for high ground. Apparently they felt trapped by the low, boggy terrain and could not just patiently wait for the wolves to disappear. The wolves responded immediately to the stampede by pursuing the herd at full speed. This chasing increased the frenzy of the stampede, and the wolves were getting exactly what they needed for a successful kill—panic from their prey. Unfortunately, I had reason to share in this feeling of panic.

By pure luck the herd was heading straight toward me. All I could do was hunker down and hope to avoid being trampled. As the herd broke around me, thundering by on both sides, one of the wolves grabbed a calf by its leg, tore at it, and separated the calf from the herd. As the wolf held on with its jaws, the calf bucked and kicked fiercely, struggling to get loose.

The rest of the pack was in pursuit of a second calf, but the herd reached high ground and closed ranks into a circle. Several pack members grabbed the second calf's leg, but the mother

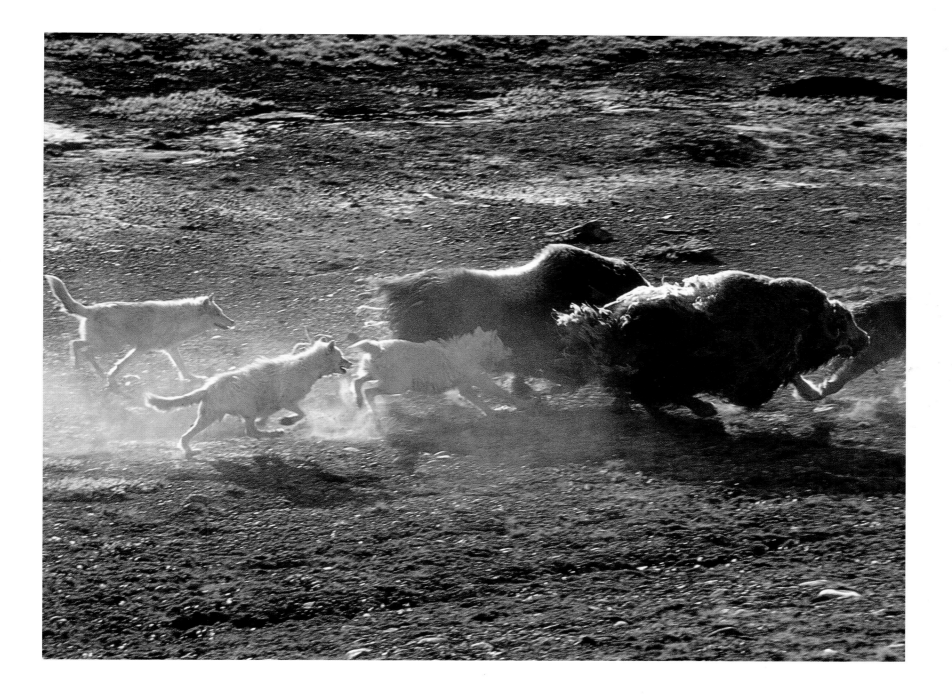

Once a kill is made, the alpha pair eats first, followed by Mom (shown here), and then the others, in the pack's descending order of hierarchy.

A doomed calf is pulled down to its death.

swung her horns wildly, nearly hooking one of the wolves. It took only the split second in which the wolves loosened their grip on the calf for it to scramble alongside its mother back to the ring.

But the first calf was still hopelessly separated from the herd, and now the entire pack swarmed over it, biting away and eating its flesh for several minutes until, finally, the calf fell and died.

Very quickly, the alpha pair took control of the carcass, feasting while the rest of the pack fidgeted around the edges, whining for a share. After Buster and Midback finally showed signs of having had enough, the lower-ranking members came closer and closer, cringing and begging hungrily.

But Buster played out his role as leader a bit longer. He stood over the carcass, snapping his jaws at the others while they inched forward on their bellies and tilted their heads back. They each wore on their faces a nervous kind of grin. After a while, the other wolves drew close enough to lick the blood from Buster's muzzle.

At last, the alpha pair seemed to have had enough groveling from the others, and the carcass could be divided up. There would be nearly twenty pounds of meat for each wolf, and it took the pack two hours to reduce the calf to hide and bones.

After the feast, the wolves splashed in a nearby pond, drinking and washing off some of the blood from their fur. Then they wiped themselves by rolling around on the grass. Even after all this, however, each wolf wore a blood mask for several days.

The kill was about twenty miles from the den, so they did not rest long before heading back. After all, six hungry puppies were waiting for them. I raced ahead with my equipment so I could record the next part of the feeding as well. The feast would be regurgitated for two reasons: to share the meat with the puppies and to store extra, undigested meat for future use.

At the den, the pups heard the older generation howling from

Throughout their engorgement, the wolves make trips to a nearby stream to drink the water that is necessary for digesting so much meat; they also wash the blood from their coats before it has a chance to dry and harden.

Exhausted from play sessions, Scruffy and the pups nap; a paw over the nose gives protection from the irritating mosquitoes.

several miles away. The reunion was delightful to watch. The pups wagged their tails while each adult proudly strutted about with its stomach stuffed to an almost comical degree.

With the pups squeaking and leaping up to nip at their muzzles, the adults soon regurgitated chunks of meat into the grass. The food was gobbled up greedily; the pups had only about six weeks of summer in which to fatten up enough to survive the winter.

It had been seventeen hours since Midback had awakened and howled to begin the hunt. The pack had traveled more than seventy miles, and the kill of a single calf would not be enough to last them long. But for now, the pack could curl up and slip into an exhausted sleep. Having been up for forty-eight hours straight, I did the same.

*A mighty yawn following
a ten-hour nap.*

*The adults carry chunks of meat in
their stomachs to regurgitate to the
pups waiting hungrily back at the den.*

⮞ Chapter 6

BIG BAD WOLVES?

For most people, the idea of waking up with a wolf sniffing at them is pretty frightening. In fact, the question I'm asked most often about my experience with the wolf pack is, "Weren't you scared?"

In fact, I experienced fear on only one occasion during my stay with the wolves. And this was because I had, for a moment, forgotten the importance of pack hierarchy and the signals of dominance and submission that maintain this system. I had carelessly stepped out of my proper "place" within the pack.

Late one morning, while filming with the movie camera near the den, I discovered Buster chewing on a seal pup carcass he'd either killed or found washed up on the beach. Seals are rarely killed by wolves, and this was the first time I'd seen a pack member eating seal meat. It seemed important and unusual enough to document. Unfortunately for me, Buster had dragged the carcass into a slight valley where the lighting was poor for photography.

After about twenty minutes of munching, he stood up and trotted away. Assuming he was finished with his meal, at least for the time being, I walked over to the seal to pull it into the light. It never occurred to me that Buster would be upset; I'd lived with the wolves long enough by this time to feel there was no reason to fear any reaction he might have. Big mistake.

I had broken one of the rules of wolfdom: Never take food away from another wolf. I've even seen adult wolves act in an almost submissive way to pups when they were the ones with the food. In other words, possession is nine-tenths of the law with wolves. It has to be that way in order to keep the peace in the pack.

Thinking only of my photographs, I reached down to move the carcass. Buster came toward me then, and there was no mistaking his body language. I'd come to know it as very serious: the intense look in his eyes, the ears erect and cocked forward, the tail raised, the hair coming up on the back of his neck. His shoulders stiffened and appeared to grow larger. They probably had.

I'm certain that if I had run, he would have attacked. Instead I did what must have become instinctive by that time—I dropped the seal and changed *my* body language. I became as submissive to Buster as I could be, cringing, retreating, making myself smaller and unimportant. If I'd had a tail, I would've tucked it between my legs.

Trying not to rush, I did finally make it to my four-wheeler and got out of there as fast as I could. Even then, he got on my heels and started chasing me. I'm not sure what would have happened if I hadn't had the advantage of that machine.

Did this experience make me more fearful of wolves? Not at all. I had been in danger because of my own foolish behavior, not because wolves tend to attack humans.

From that point on, I was able to get more footage of Buster, at closer range and with more comfort, than I had previously. In that encounter over the seal carcass, Buster had finally and clearly expressed his dominance over me, and I had shown him that I knew my place. Since I posed no threat, he was free to ignore me.

Buster, the alpha male, is the most suspicious member of the pack; here he strikes a typically assertive, in-charge pose.

I hesitate to dwell on this episode because wolves already have a bad enough reputation without any stories of imperiled photographers. The widely held opinion of wolves is that they are extremely dangerous. For centuries, children have been told fairy tales with wolves as the villains. Thanks in part to movies and books, the mere sound of a wolf howling in the distance is often enough to inspire terror. The wolf, in many cultures, is a symbol of evil.

This exaggerated fear of attack has caused so many wolves to be trapped, shot, or poisoned that, on many continents, they have been almost wiped out. In the United States, wolves today occupy less than 1 percent of their former territory.

The fact is that all the countless wolf–human interactions have resulted in virtually no recorded accounts of unprovoked attacks by healthy wolves. Our chances of being attacked by a fellow human are vastly greater than any risk posed by a wolf. Every major predator in North America, from mountain lions to grizzly bears, will occasionally strike out against humans without provocation, but wolves will not. I have asked a number of biologists about this, but there appears to be no logical explanation.

Facing page: The ever-confident Buster appears to take great pleasure in finding unusual situations.

As the summer draws to a close, the fur of the half-grown pups starts to whiten, beginning with their faces; once they reach full maturity, their coats will remain white all year long.